An Accounting of Days

Also by Charles Seluzicki

Elegiac

Prodigy by Charles Simic (as illustrator and contributor)

An Accounting of Days

Charles Seluzicki

The Cox Family Poetry Chapbook Series

Carnegie Mellon University Press
Pittsburgh 2024

Acknowledgments

An Accounting of Days by Charles Seluzicki is the fifth volume in The Cox Family Poetry Chapbook Series of Carnegie Mellon University Press. The Press administrators and staff express their profound appreciation to Courtney, Lisa, and Jordan Cox for their generous support.

The author would like to acknowledge and thank the editors of the following magazine for first publishing this poem:

Southern Poetry Review: "Strange Happenings on Norman Creek"

Grateful thanks to my editor Gerald Costanzo for continuing encouragement, Paul Merchant for our conversations about the arts of poetry, and Curtis Salgado for his lively knowledge of the life of lyric and music.

Library of Congress Cataloging-in-Publication Data
Names: Seluzicki, Charles, author.
Title: *An Accounting of Days* / Charles Seluzicki.
Other titles: *Accounting of Days* (Compilations)
Description: Pittsburgh : Carnegie Mellon University Press, 2024. | Series: The Cox
    Family Poetry Chapbook series | Summary: "*An Accounting of Days* gathers poems
    drawn from moments in personal history. Structurally, the poems move along a
    timeline starting with early memory and developing along the stepping stones of
    experience and aging." —Provided by publisher.
Identifiers: LCCN 2023046359 | ISBN 9780887487026 (trade paperback)
Subjects: BISAC: POETRY / American / General | LCGFT: Poetry.
Classification: LCC PS3619.E46845 A65 2024
LC record available at https://lccn.loc.gov/2023046359

Book design by Emily Stark

ISBN 978-0-88748-702-6

10   9   8   7   6   5   4   3   2   1

Contents

Prefatory

Always,
Gaius Valerius Catullus,
it was you,
teasing the reluctant blossom
that some call elevated speech
with a breezy flow
whose nimble transits seek
respite and, yes, at times revenge.
City fathers and other nitwits
confuse this with vulgarity.
I wonder if they were ever capable
of an honest emotion,
even as brats at home.
On hot afternoons,
the shaded spot out back
has always been the place
where you can sip cooled wine.
It is there that we can talk
of loved ones and the vacant and the false-
floods of feeling dancing on our tongues.

Strange Happenings on Norman Creek

The house was a cellar full of muskrats
grinding into the bedrooms
in those first summers. Crab pots
bobbed between oyster-gray boats
off the evening wharves of Norman Creek.

Each pot had its spooky chicken's head
laced with display case efficiency
at the end of wire mazes, or was baited
with cryptic grandfather eels who squirmed
to death in the Captain's salt-rock barrel:

Either did just as well and was just as hard
to understand, even after seeing bluefins
pinch and muzzle the pinched meat
with mandibles running like John Deere harvesters
busting in the crops on late summer afternoons.

Once past the smell, opportunities
for caged observation were for certain—
all before rattling crabs down to close boards,
claws scraping wires, holding on spread eagle
like children on centrifugal rides, or scuffling

back to meat.
            Years later I stop dead in the middle
of my rattling. Old muskrats
empty out of the bulkheads. Loose crabs plop
overboard in pairs as slow-born tidewaters
furrow the shore with impatient deathwatches.

Florida Vignettes, 1957

I

Early morning coastal gray
broken by pastel pinks and blues,
coquinas tumbling in the surf,
our youth keeping time with the tides—
Look! Look at this one!

II

Brown River evening heat,
a flotilla of shrimp,
bioluminescent in the moonlit waters.
If there had been music,
we would have held our ears.

III

Orange groves bordering
irrigation ditches, shallow
and reptilian.
We are warned of danger.

Further down the road,
a sign before the turn off:
Orange Juice
All You Can Drink
25 cents

IV

Key West.
We stop and try to take it in—
this is where Route One ends.
Just before lunch,
first intimations of Cuba.

V

Mating coral snakes
indifferent to the fire engine,
the sheriff's gut
or his imperious shotgun.
How the warnings sounded
and townspeople gathered!
It all happened at the crossroads
we called town.
I might not have understood
defiance
and how wild and colorful it might be.

VI

On hands and knees along the water's edge,
buckets full of sand fleas.
                    And an instant,
a wood stork,
looming large and primal.
By the time my eyes met my sister's,
it was gone.
Now I wonder at the visions
of children
and the stork's nearest relation,
the ibis,
ancient patron of scribes.

When in the After as Before

PUT ON YOUR COSTUMES

I remember the Formica table in the kitchen
on Lombard Street. Father sat there on Saturday
afternoons listening to "Live from the Met,"
humming to himself, I would learn, as
his father did when the boy was still Casimir Ignacy.
Vesta la giubba. This tangled privacy—
the sorrows of Pagliacci, the solace of God's love.
You are not alone. The streets are paved with gold.
Go, children, it's curtain call.

Being Born

Sometimes I stop and turn, Mother,
three days labor, the stainless forceps
marked my skull. So it began.
All things nascent, converging.

The old family house made new again.
Grandfather John and his consumptive wife,
Catherine, laid out in the living room.
That time when the living kept company with the dead.

Sometimes I stop and turn, footsteps running
backwards into the eroding light and time's enemies,
all things elemental. It is August again.
My birthdate, the origin and holding point.

TRUST

He stood in the surf with me
balanced on extended arms,
an offering to the Atlantic.
Trust your breath. Think
of everything that floats.
Driftwood, messages in bottles,
container ships and catamarans.

Trust your breath. Breathe deeply
then let go, slowly let go.
How the waves lifted me up
and returned me to his arms!
I do not remember the moment
that his arms fell away. Waves
emptied me onto the landlocked dray.

Becoming

Father, you were the second son, forever
haunted by the Old World Order.
Riven by the monotony of necessity
and the Depression's ceaseless panics,
it tested you without mercy. We all
had to learn to cope. When mother said
it was time to have "the talk," I said
that I knew and let you off the hook.

Earlier, walking hand in hand with you
down Lombard Street. With every year
that pride deepens like a distant storm
brightening with electric glee.
It was 1951.
            The early show at the Broadway
was *Pinocchio*. After, returned to light,
we rubbed our eyes. Oh, the lacey ironwork,
the cobblestones!
            Yes, I was a real boy.

Love, Plain and Fancy

A QUESTION

All this talk about love, about kisses—
the questions smell of resin and my complaint
is just as ancient. I would simply like to state
that she had finally left. I would have thought
Venus was busy with the young. Who is the god,
the goddess of flint and falling stones? For
when we fell into each other's arms, it was fire.

LAMENT

It has been three years and I am still uncertain
if I am insulted or amused by the startled,
slack-jawed lurch of the woman on the bench.
Yes, I was older but we were happy.
Maybe I should not have taken notice.
As she fell back, the arm of a timeworn metronome,
I thought, "This cannot last."
And now that I recall, "What a bitch.
Didn't your parents teach you anything?"

Duchampian Quatrain

That Ionian breeze on the Pacific shore.
Your eyes testament. Less is more.
When I touched your lips, your hair,
doors flew open, my bride stripped bare.

That Shimmering
an Aubade

As you, my dear, and I
sit here, drawing eye to distant eye,
over buttered toast and questions of stress,
I must betray a certain urge to digress,
be a little biological and surmise
that *some* creatures, unbeholden to the golden sunrise,
are quite happy to eat, to lie and luminesce.

An Accounting of Days

The account
Accumulating layer and angle
Face and profile,
50 years of snapshots . . .
　　　　　—Robert Lowell, "Our Afterlife I"

Love,
your deference
to the rosary
of implacable sorrows
grew tiresome
as blighted fruit
in unforgiving seasons.
We were falling ill.

Decades knew happiness.
Those kisses
before the luggage hit the floor,
the scarlet veil,
your fingers
loosening the buttons
of your blouse.

I reach for my pen,
recording the moments,
the careless interludes
at times oblique
as original sin
and how we suffered for it.

THE DISASTERS OF LOVE

The lure of happiness,
fellow traveler, those slowing steps
around the sun
trace a scrabble board eulogy
for each former self,
for every turn
in our maze of mirrors.
Who goes there?
My former selves try to sort it out—
the young man who overheard
his perplexed date complain *he didn't
even try to kiss me* or perhaps
the elder statesman of heartbreak
and the last rapture
consulting his echo
and the current phase of the moon
before turning over the engine.

Swallows

for James Wright

> *"Six or seven swallows drag the air*
> *Their fast play of flight unbroken*
> *As if by a voice—"*
> *—from Robert Lowell's "A Burial"*

It broke my heart, James,
your handlers in tow.
They propped you up.
One disturbance,
that terrifying silence,
in the evening's flow.
You knew that the audience
had come to hear your best.
The Venice poems
lay in the future.
I would have liked to have known you then,
your noblest self,
adrift in endless nights of midnight pacing,
reciting Trakl.
We spoke the night we met
as you struggled to write my name
inscribing your *Collected*.
The third time was the charm
as you patiently x-ed out the errors
and called me your friend.

Grasshopper Blues

Grasshopper
Grasshopper
Your distant chirp

Grasshopper
Grasshopper
Such a lonesome note

Grasshopper
Grasshopper
What did I do wrong?

Grasshopper
Grasshopper
Such a lonesome song

Oh, Grasshopper
Grasshopper
It's too dark to see

Grasshopper
Grasshopper
Can I sing along?

(SONG)

Oh my world is upside down
I look this way and that
The world is spinning round and round
Can't tell front from back
So difficult to contemplate
Such an awful state
Everyone has gone to town
And I'm just running late
I'm just running late